T0193365

# POEMS,RHYMES
# *&*
# REAL HEARTFELT SHIT

by George

authorHOUSE®

AuthorHouse™
1663 Liberty Drive
Bloomington, IN 47403
www.authorhouse.com
Phone: 1 (800) 839-8640

Published by AuthorHouse  01/07/2020

ISBN: 978-1-7283-4006-7 (sc)
ISBN: 978-1-7283-4013-5 (e)

Print information available on the last page.

This book is printed on acid-free paper.

I'm a real man with a lot of real shit to say.
I write how I feel and I've aired out my thoughts
in an interesting fun way.
These writings vary from deep shit to funny
shit, personal shit to serious shit.
Some take you away, some make you think,
some are predictable, others are unexpected.

If you're easily offended, this compilation isn't for you.
Close the book and walk away. Maybe go eat a yogurt or
some veggie sticks and call your grandma to tuck you in.

# Table of Contents

# **Destiny**

The wise man said, "Before you're dead, gravitate to
a new elevation, find your destination. Levitate your
dreams and nurture aspirations, hold them in respect
to your own preservation and internal revolution for
as long as you need, even if you can't breathe. dig in
your heels where it feels like you belong. Be strong,
unless you're in eternal rest, be my guest, swing for
the fences, no second guesses. Dare to rise above, but
accept the losses. Cursed are the trials, but blessed are
the rewards. Come forth, try at least, but try you must.
Be a beast until you turn to dust. Be driven, rehabilitate
the idle demon. Facilitate and stop the bleeding. Drink
to the success of trying. Forget losing, remember
dying with empty hands, full of regret and plans.
Blaze trails for the rest, be the best you can be.
That might just be good enough to breathe."
He's right you see; no matter what's been done to me,
I must move on and find a new victory, something
to drive me. I've lost ferocity, gone is the velocity,
I have to shake this idle feeling of reeling in self
inflicted wounds from poor inner philosophy.
Doesn't matter what was done to me.
I've let it stifle me, relentlessly, needless to say,
it's been killing me.
I need an inner victory, around this complacency.
Honestly, there's no room, for the gloom and doom and
in truth that tears us apart like new life from the womb,
it's my mind, my body and my soul to groom. Create a
new goal to bloom. Make my destiny, just like the old man
said to me, because right now- my hands are empty.

## Lighthouse

Through dark, treacherous nights, even through
the foggiest of our times, across miles of confusion
and oceans of madness, there was a constant
we knew we could all count on to be strong and
lead us to safety. Always battered and beaten, we
could still rely on a light to show us the way.
No one ever went hungry or knew how bad the
storms actually raged outside of our steadied ship.
The end of the world could have been knocking on
our windows and we would never have known.
Rare to show another side other than the
one that stood facing the storm...
we took for granted the beacon that lit our way;
and Today,
I buried that man...
My father, the lighthouse to us all. May he find
his way to wherever he's going with all of our love
lighting the way. Thank you for your courageous
strength in getting us to the next sunny day.

(dedicated to Robert E. Long)

## In my sleep

I close my eyes and drift while she lays next to me. My mind believes it's wandering deep into scenes even races and takes me to places I've never been... I'm alive where mountain tops touch blue skies, where eagles fly until their soar is so high only stars can guide their majestic flight. Waves crash into sandy shores from oceans unexplored. I see swaying trees feed the breeze their seed, whispering secrets through falling leaves. I can only imagine what it would be like to touch all of these as I breathe in deep sleep. In the distance I hear music's sweet sound kiss the air and carry me to another scene of beauty so fulfilling, a woman standing on a hill waving intently, her eyes ever so gently caress my worry and transform my anxiety into ease...once again, I can breathe. This is all a dream, it has to be, she's so beautiful it can't be real as I can feel her heat, her warmth, her love, touch my soul and then I realize it's her that's given me back the ability to feel whole and dream. She's so amazing she even guides me in my sleep.

## Ascension

The moment she pulled me close, I fell dizzily into her
beautiful pose. It was new to me, such beauty beyond
understanding and far beyond anything I had ever hoped.
Pure of heart were her intentions, as she looked into
my eyes, she gave herself to me in trust. Unafraid, she
playfully fed our lust, affection. Unaware of the growing
emotion which would soon become my new obsession.
Reading me in taunting heat, I fell into her embrace so
deep. She noticed, but denied retreat as she delivered a
unique attention so strong, words played on my lips
between kisses of bliss,
I thought to myself, is this wrong? Because
this feels like something I would miss. Words I
would never think to mention or imagine or even
dismiss, ran through my head during our physical
ascension. And then, like a freight train coming to
the end we stopped to breathe, taking it all in.
I thanked the heavens above for I believe I've met the one
I could never get enough of, the girl of my dreams,
this woman it would seem was sent from above,
an angel I would now love.

## Under starry sky

Under starry sky
mix dark blue, black and white,
oceans of serenity flood and reclaim the breezy night.
I wonder what she's doing this very minute
beyond the distance of sight.
For those deep in sleep, dreams plant seeds, break cycles,
summon and inspire new beginnings, new leases, new life.
I sigh. I still wonder what she's doing tonight
Under starry sky.
You're beautiful majestic and controlling. You've given
hope and guided. You've watched birth to death, seen
it all and yet remain the same. You've never changed.
As I sit, I ask one favor of you starry sky.
Please watch over her and her plight. Don't let her ever
think she's alone during the night. Let the moon broadcast
it's blaze and bring her hope of the upcoming light.
Until I see her again, thank you and Goodnight.


## Sharing

Sharing meals, sharing thoughts, sharing time,
a soulful trust between two shall bind and intertwined
they shall become, for a trust this strong is rare to find.
"I have a grand design" he exclaimed,
"but riddled with flaws its only ever been."
She took a look at his torn tapestry of thoughts
and deeds and within minutes she saw where the
journeys lead. She pointed out a path he had never
seen and led him to the road of successful dreams.

## <u>Two breaths</u>

In one breath I watched my entire life play by me
like an old time reel to reel. It was in a dream, but I knew
it was more than just wandering thoughts in deep sleep.
There were no voices, no one else around; just me, the
world from the breezy sunny seaside cliff on which I stood,
and time. My time. It had passed.
I've felt alone before and it's deep exhausting haunting
cold... but this was an utter relaxed alone... no pain.
As I watched the waves from afar, quietly crashing
against the rocky shore... I couldn't help wondering
what was my next journey. Up til now I had battled
every dark and demon this life could throw at
me. I was scarred, but not in pain... Worn, but
not broken... It was from what I could tell,
a new day in the dream, and then I finished my breath.
Suddenly, as if waiting for me to inhale, I felt the warmth
of a hand enter mine. Without looking I felt a confidence
come over me that this was my second chance to breathe.
I took in that gift of another deep breath
and knew it was time to make the next reel.

## Honey and almonds

Sweeter than fresh spring rains was
the honey from our hives. It was a gift to be alive in a
time where we counted on the little things to survive.
We brought our jars of the wonderful meadow
blend to the church on the corner of 'Picket's
End'. At the fair we received such praise for
the most sensational dessert of the day.
And it stayed that way until Julia James, the girl of my
dreams, the air of my breathe, the stitch in my seams
brought her magnificent warm array of snacks.
It wasn't til I bumped into her that I finally
mustered the courage to chat.
I asked her what she had, she said she felt she was
missing something to complete her spread, "If only I had
something sweet to compliment my deeds." This was my
chance to be seen. I've thought of roses, fresh biscuits and
hand crafted creams. The girl of my dreams has asked for
what I think she means ...My sweet honey ... It would seem.
I ran around as fast as I could to give Julia James the
compliment to her goods. And then it hit me. This may
not be my time to shine... as I saw Danny Cranston
down in his mind. He adored Julia more than my
meadows loved the sun, more than Gatsby loved
Daisy, more than... Well more than me, in sum.
Danny had a stove top simmering his fare,
keeping his treats warm as they filled the church air.
I brought Danny my last jar and whispered in his ear
this was his chance to appear, to save the day with his
roasted delights. I watched Danny perk up and go to
Julia's side and share what was in his bowl as I cried.
I knew it was the right thing to do,
Danny was happy and Julia smiled too.

## A Love Story

Once upon a time there was a love story so grand it had to
be shared and forth told all across the land. It began with
a beautiful loving princess, who had been abandoned and
left to walk in her distressed world, alone. Her nights were
filled with heartbreak, emptiness and tears, but it didn't
keep her from praying for her prince charming to appear,
to save her heart from the darkness that had crept in over
the passing years. And although heart torn, exhausted and
worn, she gave everything she had to protect and nurture
her loved ones through every dark day and every storm.
Not far away, a handsome young King; big-hearted and
brave, fought gallantly and gave, all he could to those he
would save, but lost was his kingdom to those he trusted
most. Bruised and battered from battles he faced, he
led a life of sadness and solitude in his fall from grace.
One day the princess wandered into the town's fair.
She heard there was courtship there. Upon arrival
she saw; kingsmen, warriors and knights lining up to
find a princess for whom they would fight. But who
would be worthy of her love, her honor, her beauty, her
heart. They needed to have more than just claimed
victories on chart. She searched and scoured, but
she knew what she wanted and most of all, needed,
it wasn't any of these men, no matter how hard they
pleaded. Her search then led to the end of a path, and
with starlight in her eyes, through a forest of lies,
she came to a clearing where only a voice exists.
There stood a man, praying to God with nothing but
a torch in his hand, but she noticed it's flame had lost
its persist. Hesitant to approach, she sharpened her
guard, curled her fingers and prepared for the worst.
She shouted to the man in the shadowy dark,
"Who are you and what is your curse!?"

Never turning to show his scars, the man overcome
with neglect, heard her voice and replied in depth,
"It is with a heavy heart I travel this far. For what
I seek cannot be found near or far. It's rare and
holds the key to my salvation. It's a beauty and a
wonder even God himself can attest; If a man find
and conquer such a quest he shall be rewarded
with enough love to fill ten hearts in his chest."
The man paused. She uncurled her fists and tilted
her head. He turned with tears on his cheeks, his
burnt torch in one hand and a gift in the other.
"What's in the box?" She asked the weary wanderer.
He declared in a broken voice;
"My heart. For I came this far not for me, but to
give my last love to the woman of my dreams.
She deserves all I can be and all that I am. I don't
need more than enough love but for one man."
The starry eyed princess placed her hand on the young
king's heart and said, "I can fill that chest with all the
love you want. I am beauty. I am rage. I am all this
world's fortune and can set your cold heart ablaze."
The King understood, raised his hand and replied in tune,
"Then I shall carry this torch... for you."

## <u>Bricks</u>

For all that we are, we can analyze how we've come this
far. The little boy that feared the dark grew up to carry
the strongest flashlight in the park. The little girl that
watched her siblings go hungry, saved her money and filled
her entire pantry. We all carry our past, it's who we are.
Our thoughts are not faults, weaknesses, or ticks, they're
gaps we fill in with homemade bricks to rise above and
protect us, from the storms that will break us and leave us,
stranded. It's best to understand it, so we can command it,
and control our future selves, better, to the letter and never
judge a person with less or how they insist they dress,
it's most likely a reaction from the past
that has affected their present tense.

## In their eyes

What kind of man would I be to let a child go hungry?
They look up to me, love me, make me laugh and cry,
but believe in more than just me.
They believe in the power of the almighty grown up.
So it's for us to own up.
It's almost magical in theory, their assumption that
we can protect and save them from anything scary.
Our word is gold, but our teachings are held
as the highest commodity.
We're amazing In their eyes.
We're all they have to survive.
We're as tall as trees and stronger than steel.
We rescue them from fears and wipe away their tears.
With eyes so wide, how could I ever live with myself
if I turned my back and just let them cry or lose
faith inside or even God, why? I'd just die.
Are there really reasons why a man could
just ignore a child's life?
I shouldn't have to explain to any man how to treat a child.
You should know or die by the darkness they fear in the
wild. I have zero forgiveness in me, but as you can see,
I must now run and save my son from the monsters in
his head and teach him he's the most powerful being
under the sun, and remind my miniature friend,
I'm here til whatever God declares, 'the end'.
Until then, let's take up swords and together
we'll fight the demons under your bed.

## More than a kiss

She said, "Let's meet for a kiss tonight." The kiss
that had burned inside both of them for what
seemed like an eternity in flight. Their words
carefully chosen to fan the sparks of their new found
destiny. Time taught them how to climb the vines
of hope along the treacherous cliffs of agony.
But alas, seemed as though hope had been dying for some
time and it's flames have twisted below the rocky pile of
dreams and security. But this kiss was a fight for eternity.
Eternity was the wind under the flame,
the muse for the heat.
A magic that would transport her, save her, change his and
her lives forever. His strength would wash away her fears.
He could taste her tears running down her cheeks and
this moment on their lips promised an eternity of bliss.
And like angels dancing in the sky their kiss made a love
that twisted a new vine on which they could both climb,
stepping over broken dreams and planting new seeds
in the mountain of hope they shared in their minds.
All this was in their kiss, but a kiss is never just a kiss.
It was always more than just a kiss.

## <u>Black Cloud</u>

Here I stand in silence, the years have come and gone.
The road; old and worn has left only a tired memory
and all that once was and all that once delivered me,
are gone and abandoned just like the promises of dreams.
No I never meant to drag you down.
There's an evil pulling us under only heaven knows.
Heaven knows- why.
I'll never forget the hardest thing that I ever did. This life
has always been a picture of drowning in hopelessness.
No I never meant to drag you down.
There's an evil pulling us under- only heaven knows.
Heaven knows.
And I wrestle with the whole world for what
they've done to you,
but there's a wickedness in the air,
my black cloud of despair.

(dedicated to Marc A. Tedesco)

## We Drown

There's nothing more terrifying than drowning.
We drown in our own self pity.
We drown in our politics, our beliefs, our debt,
our lies and our failures.
We drown in our loneliness and sorrow.
We drown in our own stagnant pool of the go nowhere
tomorrow. Same is said about burning alive,
yet the burning inside to fuel the fire that drives our inner
machine to succeed at our dreams and desires can also
backfire as we chase those dreams too far and too high
and ride to close to the sun, passing what was once fun
and incinerating our sanity and financial ability,
even trying the patience of humanity in the ones around
us such as family. We forget everything and everyone
around us and finally, drown in our obsession.
Let this be a lesson, dream far, love hard, live wise,
just don't let your goals become your demise or
drown in their overwhelming disguise.

## Seasonal hurt

Were those sessions- real confessions? Have you learned
your lesson or is it just you messin' around to lessen the
guilt, its the way you're built to bury the mistakes you're
too proud to admit that possess you and control you,
borderline - own you. I'm guessin' it's the latter, but it's
a blessing to wake up free of lies and see the light, no
matter how much fight you had to go through. It's better to
wake up 'black & blue' instead of six feet under like you've
never existed or hiding behind a disguise, conflicted.
Not sure what I expected. I was neglected, fragile
and dissected yet still connected to my mind's eye.
It's all-knowing, in time; growing to accept without
rhyme or reason, it seizes the way it was designed
to work to get through the seasonal hurt.
So forget the pain. It'll be back again, but until then,
I'll be ready to sustain what remains. It's certainly
a challenge to play this game unafraid.
This is my life, this is my refrain.

## Realign

This is not a song or a story. This is not a game that
offers second chances. Last I checked in we were trading
fake glances, you were fading away, down on your luck,
broken dreams, falling apart at the seams, on your
knees, begging the world to please, stop spinning.
You were constantly laying blame on others why
you weren't winning. Last time I found you, you were face
down in hurt, in so much pain it felt like you'd been cursed
from birth. Or is it all the bad decisions you make day after
day, year after year and have no one to blame but yourself
for the failure level you maintain, then wonder why you're
drowning in a pool of your own tears again and again.
I'm sorry, I know the truth hurts, but hiding from it
or denying it won't help break the curse.
It's a new day, find a new way, the mirror never lies.
Realize, reclaim and Re-align.
Wake up and redesign your life. Start with your mind.
Change your thinking from the ground up, because you're
the only one that can fix this shit that is so fucked up.

# He is not my son

He is not my son. I may look in his eyes and see myself-
a young boy inside, with hopes and needs that have
been pushed aside and denied, but he is not my son.
I may be in his life, his mother, my wife,
but he is not my son. I only nurture this little boys soul,
pat his back and fill his belly, bond with him over
laughter, and tuck him in after we've been silly and tell
him he's been a good boy because I'm a grown man,
I'm sure he understands.
He may smile at me, hug me, even love me,
but he's another man's responsibility, and
that's clearly what the boy believes.
He doesn't want to call me Daddy. If he wakes up with
needs, like clothes or shoes for his tiny feet, it's not my
problem. He may come to me when he's sad, even look
at me like I'm a God who can solve every problem with
just a wave of my hand.
But he is not my son... He is more than that.
He's a gift that has made me whole, balanced my mind and
soul and taught me more than I ever thought I needed to
know. And even though he is not my son, I've never looked
at him in any other way. I love him no less than a mountain
and more than the furthest reaches of my dreams.
I'm forever lucky to have been a part of his life and
can imagine this is how a proud father feels.

## **Disgraceful**

Erase all disgraces. Wash away the remains of our
stasis. Imagine days where our greed and lust for
power and places, riches and pretty faces don't burn
bridges and chase away what amazes and gives us
everything we've ever needed instead of torched in
blazes, torn apart into pieces, used til there's no traces.
This life, these lands, the beauty around us, that is us,
is now a circus. A loveless, selfish, sin filled fortress.
It's inexcusable, and shameless, irresponsible and
hopeless. it's unacceptable as it is inescapable.
We'll never change. We're incapable.
We're always on the brink, we're always being warned,
we think who the fuck we are, we're too good to be
scorned. A lesson learned is a dead man mourned.
Soon it'll be too late to overturn and we'll all be asking
why while we all slowly burn; a death deservedly earned.

## The Devil's due

You're making me go a place I've buried deep
where sinister sinks it's claws into memories.
Innocence was lost along the way.
The harder the road, the further the light will be.
All my life, I've walked through fire.
I've fought the night just to make it to the next light.
So ya think ya know real pain.
Walk a mile in these shoes, I've already bled in.
Just don't blink, the crow's at it again,
pickin' apart your world of woes.
Deep in the broken heart, darkness grows.

Take a long look at the so called God-fearing man.
He rises only to fall to the tempting hand.
It's mind-numbing, fuck coming up with a plan,
we're still gonna lose
I've been shot six times through the heart,
give the devil his due.
Sad is the truth.

Terrified from the eyes in the mirror.
Recognize all the tears have a reason.
In your mind with the lies and the secrets.
All alone and the darkness feeds it.

Hear the cries in the silence growing.
Have we done all we can with our voices
After all of the damage taken,
Can we climb a new high and reverse it?

## The Tale of the Miserable Fuck

This is the tale of the miserable fuck. Just a short story about a real prick. A piece of work in every way. He would talk shit about everyone under his breath, every fucking day. This fake ass piece of miserable shit betrayed and played as if he was doing the right thing by ratting every chance he got, about anything that seemed off to him, no matter what. He overstepped his position and made an opposition of every man around him because everything had to be his way.

One day a patient man, a saint as he was known, recognized the traits of the old miserable, cock sucking bag of bones and tried a new angle. He approached him with kindness and gestures and invitations to family dinners- suspecting the miserable fuck had no one left to love, no one to share life with or even speak of. Of course the saint's suspicions were true. That old miserable fuck had lost everything he ever knew. He became injured and depressed, not a woman nor a child or even a friend would ever come through. So the saint continued his mission of kindness with belief that one day through the years, the old man would be brought to tears and see the error in his ways. Well, after many years of hellos and good mornings, gifts and genuine greetings, the saint had reached a point to speak about his humanitarian connection and called a meeting.

"Gather 'round good gentlemen, I have something to say, as God is my witness on this very day, I've done my very best to find a better way to communicate and after years of hard work that I did so dedicate, it's my job as a saint to tell you all what I've learned before its too late. He's not a miserable fuck. Please don't call him that, He's a gargantuan, miserable fucking cunt. I've tried everything except shooting him in the face. There's no hope for that bigoted piece of dog shit disgrace.

He's an absolute backstabbing twit. A know it all, sac of monkey shit. A moron without brain "one" in his fucking head and there's zero chance to connect with him cuz he's most likely inbred. Let's all pray that miserable fuck falls down a flight of stairs, breaks every bone in his body and dies today. God bless everyone, except that miserable fuck and have a great day.

## Man

In all Man's wisdom he can't escape the chasm under the tightrope on which he walks. There are many paths to choose, but it wouldn't be human to be prudent and travel secure. It's the allure of power, success, money and pleasures that man is attracted and treasures. when pooled together, his thoughts and efforts have conquered and climbed, overcome and survived, but dangle riches and material possessions and it's the true beast inside that shows his obsession with temptation. Even with haunting dark depths below, knowing its impossible to walk back across the rope with stolen thrones, bloodied hopes and ransacked dreams, he still reaches for that which doesn't belong to him. He'll always have the same outcome and perish in his breach.

## Everyone's a Critic

Rhyme less, rhyme more, everyone is a connoisseur.
Be straight forward, Be more diverse, but
beware, sounding pretentious is worse. Be
real, don't say whatever you want, but say how
you feel. You're talented, you're a hack,
you're inspiring, you're crazy.
You're not my type, you amaze me.
Too many chefs- not enough kitchen.
Don't worry about how my brain thinks, just listen.
I don't write for you or attention, I write for relaxation
and mental preservation.
If you're curious about my conviction and want
a connection, hesitate to give your opinion,
it means less to me than a sentence that doesn't rhyme.

I don't need validation for expression.

# Greatest moment of my life.

Never had I seen anything more precious nor had I known
anything so amazing. To this day I'm still in shock at
what the good Lord gave me. Until that moment, my eyes
had never been so wide. Suddenly she was in my arms
and I swear I saw her smile. My heart instantly melted.
Tears ran down my cheeks as I cried. Carefully I held the
most important, most beautiful thing I had ever known
in my life. In a flash I became independent and whole,
my existence had new meaning as she became the driving
force behind every goal. But she needed me to be more
than just me. She needed a guardian angel to protect her,
a hero, and a Daddy who would never neglect her. It was
a job and a title I was more than happy to make mine.
She'll always be my little girl even when she becomes
a wife, she is and will always be the love of my life.

## Some say

Some say prepare for the worst, its a shit show at best.
Some say it's a curse, like getting fucked in the ass first-
no dinner, no kiss. A brutal dissection, with constant
interrogation, zero affection, loss of connection.
Emotional constipation,
what's the point of this conversational direction,
where's the lesson?
Well, others say
it's better to never surrender,
remember your time together, the time you met her,
the time you fed her, the intimate pleasure,
the time she made you wear that stupid fucking
sweater. Don't give up or think you're clever.
Whatever the cause is, navigate your voices, there's choices,
fix broken promises. Repair no matter what the cost is.
It's easier to fill a heart with love than losses.

# Dirty, old black man

Quiet man, kept to himself. Hardest working man I've ever known. 'Toot', is what he told us to call him. I've never seen hands so dry and worn, calloused and gray. Just looking at his thin, old, five foot nine frame, made me wonder how he did it every day. With a hot breakfast sandwich, coffee and orange juice for him, I'd pick up Toot from the train station every time I ran a jobsite, new construction, but only on the first day. He made his way to the sites after the initial ride. All the men had cars and trucks, but Toot just asked to be dropped off at the train station nearby. He never said much more than that and we never asked why. One day someone thought they saw a man on the site, light on, inside. I assumed it was kids until it was reported back to me, it looked like a dirty, old, black man, immediately said to myself in shock, "Toot? No fuckin' way. I dropped him off at the train earlier today." My mind was firing through so many questions. My jaw on the ground. I hastily drove back in the freezing cold, that night and staked out the site. It was late. To be honest I was scared. I was alone, far away from the safety and warmth of home. I saw light and movement so I quickly ran into the new house. The distinct sound of my work radio was on, now I was even more nervous. I heard water running so I pulled out my hammer and opened the bathroom door. There was Toot, almost naked except for boxer shorts, barefoot on the hard floor, washing his socks in the sink. It dawned on me, Toot never had a home or any place to go. Took a shower and washed his clothes. His backpack and blanket with a job site heater on the tile.

He just looked at me.
I almost cried. So much I wanted to say, but I just flat smiled and with a nod salute, I pulled the door shut and said, "Goodnight, I'll see you tomorrow, Toot."

## <u>Your Story</u>

I have to share this yearning, this dreaming during
the day, this relentless feeling of you stirring inside
me, running through my head, rummaging through
a collection of my past rejection. Effortlessly you
take the breath outta me with this affection you
give to me. Truthfully, it feels heaven sent, even
though we just met. I know this is crazy.
Nevertheless I must tell you, I have to confess
I'm drowning in your stare. You glare like bright
blinding rays off the ocean.
You radiate like magnificent suns in motion
and you're just sitting there.
My soul, is naked and bare, exposed
to the air of you reading me, seeing me for all that I
am, including my vulnerability, but our connection
beams joyfully. Spiritually we comprise this part
of our journey, as we join forces.
We weave love into the story of our lives
with the choices we make to find and share all that we are.
To be a part of your glory, this new energy is an
unexpected fulfillment with our synergy and has crept
down deep into my core, like never before. I want more.
Honestly, I crave this unity and
happy to have found myself there,
in your story.

## Recognize

A real man recognizes his journey.
Whether it's one of failures or successes,
he can clearly see where
he's made mistakes and where he's flourished.
However, it is said that every man will fail to see where
he should be ashamed and where he should be proud.
'Riches' do not make successes.
Nor should riches make you proud.
'Lack of' does not equate to failure
or warrant pity or shame.
Failures don't mean you've failed,
nor does there have to be blame.
There are no medals for trying,
but winning does not mean you've won.
It takes a real man to recognize;
we all have different obstacles to overcome,
and we don't all have the same race to run.


## Watery Grave

Tears cried, tears saved, time is a watery grave.
Lives lost, souls betrayed, bury your brother or daughter,
a stranger or mother, its all the same. Stand for what they
died for, live for what they fought for, but don't forget
the tears they've cried, how alone they were inside,
how hard they tried and now that they've died,
we can fight and overcome.
Tell them sorry for all that we've done,
but it'll never drain all the tears time has collected unsung.

## Tunnel Vision

A mission discovered. A goal uncovered, a version
of existence has met resistance, but it's the reason
for breathing, completes the being, competes with
feeling, retreats and beliefs of fleeing are unfavorable,
unfathomable, unrelatable, and unforseeable and most
definitely unacceptable at this level. A vision born, is a
goal underway. A vision scorned cannot be torn apart or
led astray. Sacrifices of epic proportions will be made.
Just as the plant grows toward the sun or the tide fights
the clock to rise, I wake with magnetic blood drawn
to climb the mountain I see in my sleep.
A goal I must keep.
With every breath I believe.

## Dear Brother

A young man looked up to his older brother like he was just the greatest thing to be. He adored him and frankly was loved back equally. But it didn't stop the older brother who knew better, than to use and abuse in front of a mind so susceptible, pliable and gullible. There's no way he could handle something so combustible, the empty promises, the dirty hand of the demon reaching into his throat to claim the heart of him. It's inevitable, he'll get in and wreck him. So where was the older brother's head? Seems like he found it when his little brother was found in a way he never wanted to find him. There's no pretty way to rhyme or sugar coat his death. The broken heart and shame. The endless guilt and tears that drain every ounce of life that remain every single day. There's no easy way to say this, it's something I'll live with and take to my grave how I led a little man astray who looked up to me. How the fuck do I even say sorry.

### Dog shit

It's cute how you deceived me. Lied right to my face and believe me, it was a catastrophe, a black arrow straight through the heart of me. Let's call a spade a spade when you fucked him you changed the game, left me and the babies and then tried to say I was to blame. You left a mess in our hearts and heads, planted seeds and out the door you went. Wouldn't have been such a big deal if we weren't tied at the alter. Remember? Your sister was the witness to the kisses and promises of bliss and loyalty you so quickly dismissed? No? Well reminisce. Cuz I thought we were solid and would go on forever. All those songs you sang to me. Sade and her symphony. Blasphemy. But alas, I moved on for me and after the gutter I found another who loves me better than you ever did. You're garbage to me, pure dog shit. A bad memory, fading out, like you never existed.

## A Waste of Space

Make no mistake, this is a shallow tune, cuz there's
nothing deep about describing you, but I'll try to, go
slow for you. I'm sure you haven't a clue. You're easily
offended with a weak constitution. Congratulations, you
haven't an imagination or graduated from the institution
of self infatuation and accepted human expression. Must
be depressing, living in isolation, I'm guessing- how
everything's about how you feel, wake up, be real,
life's a blessing, just deal. start confessing, but don't
kneel. Stand up, man up, or how about just shut the fuck
up, put your hands up, like a criminal, you're abysmal.
like an itchy tickle. you're a disappointment,
you need ointment, make an appointment, to get looked at.
You're a sac-o-shit, a crack addict,
lamer than a sports fanatic-
livin' in their momma's dirty attic.
I could stand here and curse you out like I planned too,
but man that wouldn't do, any justice in labeling you.
You've made everyone's world so shitty since you
dropped out of your father's cock and popped
off your momma's titty. What a pity.
You cant hide behind phony smiles and lies, don't cry,
I'm outta time, you're a waste of space in my eyes.

## Little girl Inside

She may be a young woman,
but there's still a little girl inside.
She's in there, somewhere, maybe buried deep down
below, because the world made her grow, gave her bills
to pay, and put her on the go. Took her toys away and
life decreed she get on the fast track and leave. That
happy innocent child, the one that ran wild with an
unfettered smile, has been locked up for so long. The
little girl inside is tired and fading, crying and hating,
her life, hiding in the darkness waiting to be found and
told she can come out and be herself again. Well then,
Please come back to me, Daddy's sorry. I'll fix whatever
you need me to fix. I'll do whatever you want me to,
whatever I have to do to get you back in my arms again.
You won't have to work so hard then. Come, let me see my
little girl and tell you stories of when, we used to be- happy.
I miss you.

## Rage on

Chase your dreams, they say,
but are they tangible in any way?
Are they even your own?
Are you being told what to dream about?
And forced what to learn about?
Are you being pumped with bullshit to keep your head
in the clouds, to take your voice out of the crowds and
silence your individuality, your God given personality,
and eventually keep you occupied til you decay and
waste away the amazing gift of life on society's design to
keep you controlled in a very specific, day to day- way.

Nature didn't put a cage on us,
it made us who we really are inside.
We're climbers that thrive, travelers and explorers who've
died searching for the other side. But at least we died
trying. Not boxed up, sick and lying, forced to label each
other and our innate behavior. We're achievers at heart.
We research and investigate, but most of all creators of
our own fate and that can work in two different ways.
If we're going to eradicate, then let it be the rules
that govern our lives. Change the way we survive.
Be the preacher who believes in expanding our horizons,
get past the set ups, the spoon fed lies, and same old
environments. Lose the childish hatreds and pointless
racism and be more than what society, that's dictated by
policy, needs you to be. Solidarity is key. Unity is free.
Wash, rinse, repeat isn't for me.
Rage on, break out of the cage.
Life should be full of energy and discovery,
not complacency as a slave.

## The Stork and the Ho

Lisa was quite the Ho, well, with a name like Lisa, that's
already known. Lisa didn't care about consequences.
She would sleep with any man that crossed her path
that made promises. Throw a drink in with that and
a guy could play all day. At the ripe age of twenty
three Lisa cried in pain and begged for mercy. No,
not from S.T.D's, although she has been extremely
lucky; she had never given thought to pregnancy, until
now. News traveled fast as the stork caught wind of
her baby bump. He ran to the head stork up front.
"There's no way I'm giving that whore a kid,
she doesn't even have a home, and sucked
fourteen dicks this Tuesday alone!"
The head stork stood and said,
"Well you better get this resolved, 'cuz in no time
she'll be next on your delivery list- unless you
can prove she's outright wrong for the task, in
which case we'll give the father the kid."
On a mission, the stork called in a favor; his
friend the beaver and a donkey, his neighbor.
"Guys, I need you to let me know if that Ho
can handle this gift. If she does one more sexual thing
while this pregnancy is in, the whore ain't gettin' a kid,
the father is."
Some time had passed and the Stork went to check on
his buddies and see how they were doing. He wanted
to film her wrongful pleasures and found quite the
goings on. Lisa had become friends with the two, but the
donkey blocked the view. All he heard were the words,
"I love petting my hairy beaver and rubbing my fat ass too."
But that wasn't enough to convict. He had to catch her in
the act, catch her sucking on a dick. The stork flew in for
a closer look. That's when he tripped over the donkeys
cock, stepped on the hairy beaver and landed in her nook.

The donkey kicked and shook his fat ass, while the beaver
danced in the gook. Seems the stork landed dick first,
fell into her pussy fat and accidentally fucked her in the
kid crack.
The beaver was so shocked he yelled,
"Get a lawyer, 'cuz in about two
minutes you'll be a dirty ass,
whore fucking, father!"

## **Primrose**

I question any man who gives the silent treatment and
ignores another man. That's a bitches game you play
with your woman you brought to the big boy arena.
Don't play pussy and act like you got nothing to say,
Have a plan. Don't walk away.
Don't play politically correct
or sling shit passive aggressively.
Don't lie to me or blow smoke up my ass
or even think for a second, "I'm stupid",
because that would be a huge mistake,
like confusing niceness for weakness.
No real man can ever be offended.
So what. Grow up. Man the fuck up, you primrose cunt.
And say what you have to say.
Because this is what I've learned about the bitch
who plays silent;
It was of your doing that started the whole thing in
the first place. Something didn't go your way and
now you're butt-hurt.
You got called out on your shit and I didn't give a
fuck what you had to say. I didn't care yesterday,
and I certainly don't give a flying fuck today. That's
why I did it my way. Oh I faked it 'cuz I know deep
down you're a rusty cunt or how I'll play stupid just
to shut you up, because it's embarrassing to me
to watch a man mishandle my confrontation.
It would be too much of a realization that I manned the
fuck up, took charge and had my reasons, when you were
too busy tucking tampons in your creases.

# **Promises**

The promises we make verse the promises we keep.
It's an ongoing struggle to believe the words we speak.
So many promises made, how easily they could be
a mistake, said under pressure, said as a gesture.
said to make us feel better. So easily they slide off the
tongue, making us grand the moment they are sung.

But do we mean them?
Are they truly to be held in the highest?
They're believed without proof by both young and by
old never, in any way, having to be backed by anything
precious like silver or gold, they're created and sold.
"Don't worry", we say, "It'll be done" or "I'll be there"
and just like that, they're cast out into the air
without a thought or a care.

But what is a promise? It's a mans word. It's a man's
word saying he'll follow through. He'll come to the
rescue. He'll save the day with his promise made, but
since when has man's word ever held any value or
validity? Secondly, promises are made against the
impossible, never something simple, born out of
necessity to prevent emergency, to save just one or
to save the many, a promise is made to ease the mind.
Whether to a child or all of mankind, a promise
is a dangerous tool, believed by only a fool.

If I had a token for every promise broken,
I'd have enough to save the universe
from man and his ultimate demise, his eternal lies.

## Angry seed

Obvious in the eyes of others.
Harder to recognize in the mirror.
You'll reach depths so low, you'll wake in tears, broken
and alone, watching it take root and grow. The demons
responsible will make the festival of life impossible and
will pester and fester inside, even haunt you forever.
I've seen this first hand.
A potential demise. It's a weakness seen, draining your
life of respect and dreams. Somehow, someone,
planted this angry seed.
No one wants to be told, I get it, but giving in to loathe,
growing out of control minute by minute, you're slowly
deceived. Leaving a good soul to bleed out its lifeforce,
bowing only to a new master of seethe and grief
to steer you off course.
Ya see, bitch and moan, and complaining
about things done wrong is how it feeds.
Enraged, and bitter. You lose your temper. It's
never for the better. These aren't just words I've
strung together. This is a warning delivered.
Persuaded and tempted, you'll portray an individual
determined. Determined to become someone
unrecognizable. Vengeful, scarred and scorned,
even transform into the liar. Drug infused, perhaps
thief aspired. A mission of destruction and further
off the path 'given and desired' to travel, darkness
will grow and unravel it's vine-like fingers & hands
become dirty, decisions made, foolishly. A world
of madness will consume you. eventually.
Reconsider, when letting emotion be a leader.
Deeper into this hole I've personally wandered.
Precious time and precious life squandered.
be careful what you let grow in your garden.

## The little turtle

"Fuck off!" said the little turtle.
"Fuck off with all your tired shit. Ya know, whether I'm
poor or rich, you still could never hang with this.
Don't be oblivious. I'm sick of hearing your voice, sick
of your poor ass choices, sick of the way you walk, the
way you talk, the company you keep, how you look, how
you eat, even the sounds you make when you sleep.
You got no flava, no soul, no color, you're smothered
in muck and duller than fuck. You say I'm too fast, I'm
too slow, or maybe my shell is too fuckin' thick. How
bout sucking this fish flavored, camouflage colored,
shit-scented, dick.
There's definitely a message I'm trying to send.
Read between the lines my friend.
Your attitude is for shit so go fuck yourself
with a dick that don't bend.
I just wanna be left alone to figure out shit on my
own, But I'm sorry, you high falutin fuck, you're stuck
thinking you're so much better than me. I'm not up
to your standards it seems, but more importantly,
should I be?
I'm not as tall as the stork, or have a speckled dork,
but I'm just as brave as the lion, so don't roll your eyes
and smile like I'm a dumb-ass fuckin' rhino who hasn't
a clue or good enough for a conversation or two.
I'm just letting you know, I'm letting you go, if ever
you could see, you're not better than me in any way
shape or form. I'll just 'yes' you to death with my last

breath, til I get back home, back in my little shell, away from you all. So fuck off, and fuck you, you pretentious fucking, fuck and don't be surprised the cookies I baked for you, taste like shit squeezed from a duck."

## **Cherish**

You're truly beautiful and I mean that more than you
know, more than words can say and more than I could
possibly ever show. You're so many things rolled up into
one amazing woman. Only a god could've created such a
person. Beautiful is both inside and out, but more than
that, you take the time to show me how to be there for you,
by becoming better internally. You're guidance, advice and
clarity help break the stubborn, know it all fool inside me.
Yes, even a grown man with victories under his belt can
learn a thing or two, or three, just by opening his eyes and
hearing direction, besides the voices inside. Learning is
a constant. It never stops and should always be. It takes
a real man to see that a woman can fix his inner being.
It's my job to stay pliable. Be an old dog that can
learn new tricks, hear others out and see things from
a different perspective. Not many get that objective.
But you came and told me, showed me, inadvertently,
I needed it to be expressed soulfully, carefully...
Shown that someone cares for me.
A lot of wrong has been done to me.
I've lost faith in humanity.
I've lost faith in the women around me,
even lost faith in me, personally.
So thank you for the time you've taken to open my
eyes to your patience and love and my mistakes.
You're so much wrapped up into one.
A perfect pretty package I get to hold in my arms,
that I'll cherish 'til God calls us home.

## <u>Judged</u>

Today I was judged by a man who cares little about
himself, his looks, his hygiene, and his appearance.
He cares less about being a parent to his children than
he does about his shitty work ethic. He had a lot to say
about the things I spend my time on and take seriously.
nevertheless,
this know-it-all prick got to me.


For me to say his voice doesn't matter would be
me discounting his opinion and existence,
and pushing him away, possibly ignoring words I
should be heeding instead of judging him so intently.
but what is judging?


Well, here's what a wise man once told me.


"Set aside mighty words spoken in writings, they're
often taken out of context and don't apply to reality.
Everyone is judged and that's how we survive,
end of story.
Forget the masses that continue to harass you no
matter what mountain you climb... they're just jealous
inside. Everyone thinks they're smarter than the next
in line, that's human nature- know the creature.
The bottom line;
Would you lend this motherfucker a dime or let him
spend time with your daughter? Would you share meals
with him or fight for what he values as real? Because
his consistency and 'word kept' will set the tone on
how you should feel. Are you really judging him or just
going by his past record of how he pisses in the wind?
You know deep inside how you feel about another,
so if he ain't your brother, he's just another
motherfucker with an opinion,
and opinions are like assholes... fuck them."

## Good morning

Helloooo? I'm talking to you. How about wiping that
stupid fucking look off your face when I'm looking at
you. Is it so out of the blue that someone said hi to you?
It goes "Good morning, how are you?" Then you smile
and say, "I'm fine thank you". But you hesitated, like it
was complicated. looked at me, condescendingly. Left me
feeling awkward dare I say offended. Something so simple
turns into the weirdest moment that has now escalated.
Of course I'm agitated, I'm ground down and fucking
frustrated. No I'm not gonna calm down, like I'm some
kinda clown, with 3 heads and a fu-man-chu frown from
fun-town. Fuck this merry-go-round.
This is what's wrong with society. Not me. I simply
offered you a gift, for free, but my endeavor to
make a nice gesture, will now be labeled forever
the weirdest thing ever, because your posture and
attitude were like; whatever. You've made it impossible
for me to stay positive. Expletive, expletive, I'm so
fucking pissed and full of negative, I want a
*'smack the stupid right off your fucking face',* narrative.
But I'm thinking, there's more where that came from.
I'm sure you're so full of stupid shit it's amazing, so
much so I could wind up in front of a judgeship, with a
judgement, handing me a sentence, for this dumbshit.
Landing me in cell block, on my knees worshipping
big dick, cursing me for ever tryna show courtesy.
Next time I'll just flip this and walk on by
minding my own fucking business.
Fuck this.

## Remedy 4 a girlfriend w/a big fucking mouth

Ode to the pretty bitches with spiked tongues that spit
nasty uncalled for threats and condescending messages.
You jump to conclusions, you fly off the handle and speak
as though my wrists aren't equipped with two fucking
fists. Although I would never strike you and have never hit
a woman, it's my belief that you push and poke the bear
just to see if black and blue would match an outfit or two
or even your hair. This bear doth also have feet to walk
away, this animal could Chuck Norris his feet into your
head all fucking day. Although I would never condone such
an activity as I have patience and class, it's as if you still
want to test me and see if my hightops could polish your
pretty ass. Yes I could push you off the highest of cliffs or
just ignore your thousand and one texts. I could also buy
a bus ticket and travel real far away, but you'd still call
and call and somehow manage to fuck up my Saturday.
So whats a fella to do?
My suggestion to all of you if your bitch wakes you with
text 'one hundred and two', because you fell asleep
after working the whole week through; stop bathing,
stop washing your balls, stop paying for meals at fancy
dinner halls. Stop calling, stop talking, stop breathing
if she's near, cuz there's no way she'll want to date you if
you're quiet, poor and your balls smell like your rear.

## <u>Beings</u>

It is often forgotten and overlooked who we are and why we are here. We wake and go about our scheduled days, designed by scholars and laws that govern our ways, making sure we live in fear, driven to only achieve, driven to only follow beliefs. Slowly we walk through time to find the purpose of our lives, we count and measure successes and failures and walk a line til our eventual, individual demise. Most of us have an idea how long we have to live, learn, grow, reproduce, pass on what we know, then give in to the inevitable and die. Some of us drone on, lost in trance, others look in the mirror and have a feeling of what's beneath the skin, what electric force drives us deep within. Some deny the complexity of our existence, strongly supporting random theory of appearance, while others swear we're alien to this world sent here to discover and reveal, but most insist and get lost in the religion of existence swearing they know the answers and whom we should follow. Those fortunate to survive disease, sickness, wars afar or wars inside, will wade through bodies time has left behind and driven by a hunger to find the answers that can only be found in tomorrow. That's admirable and it's in our nature to push away and deny, but the answers we seek are already revealed and in our hands today. They lie deep inside and in the precious minutes we say we can't wait to pass us by. We're beings of love lost in sorrow, lost in a world of chaos, strife, lies and terror. Embrace today and the ones around you, because as you already know, for some, there may never be a tomorrow.

Printed in the United States
By Bookmasters